Luther Library
Midland University
900 N. Clarkson St.
Fremont, NE 68025

"Sell a country!
Why not sell the air,
the great sea,
as well as the earth?"

Tecumseh, Shawnee

RED HAWK....

For Gene Davis, generous brother and friend.
C.R.

Copyright © 1996 by The Rourke Corporation, Inc.
Text copyright © 1996 by Gloria Dominic.
Illustrations copyright © 1996 by Charles Reasoner.

Published by Troll Communications L.L.C.

Published by arrangement with The Rourke Corporation, Inc.

First paperback edition published 1998.

Printed in the United States of America.

10 9 8 7 6 5 4 3 2 1

Library of Congress Cataloging-in-Publication Data

Dominic, Gloria, 1950-
    Red Hawk and the Sky Sisters: a Shawnee Legend/by Gloria Dominic: illustrated by Charles Reasoner.
        p. cm.—(Native American Lore and Legends)
        Includes bibliographical references.
        Summary. Relates the story of the skilled hunter Red Hawk, who captures and marries the youngest daughter of Bright Star, only to have her return to the sky with their son.
        ISBN 0-86593-432-4 (lib. bdg.)   ISBN 0-8167-4514-5 (pbk.)
        1. Shawnee Indians—Folklore.   2. Tales—United States.   [1. Shawnee Indians—Folklore.
2. Indians of North America—Folklore.]   I. Reasoner, Charles, ill.   II. Title.   III. Series.
E99.S35D67 1996
398.2'089973—dc20   96-9111
                                                                                              CIP
                                                                                              AC

Designed by Susan and Dave Albers

RED HAWK

AND THE SKY SISTERS

A SHAWNEE LEGEND

ADAPTED AND RETOLD BY GLORIA DOMINIC

ILLUSTRATED BY CHARLES REASONER

Troll

Very long ago, a young man named Red Hawk lived deep within the forest. Handsome and strong, Red Hawk was a brave hunter known by all for his keen senses and skill.

Red Hawk's sharp eyes helped him to track game. He could spot and follow the trails left by deer and other animals, trails so faint that others could not detect them. And the young man's ears were able to hear the softest rustle of a bird taking flight.

Silently, Red Hawk would stalk his prey, following its path through the forest. His aim was always true. Each day he would return to his people, bearing meat for all.

With each trip he took, Red Hawk ventured further into the forest. Another hunter might have felt uneasy setting foot in a dark forest where none had gone before. But Red Hawk always looked for a more difficult trail to follow, to challenge his skills as a hunter.

One day Red Hawk found himself deep within an unfamiliar part of the forest. As he walked on, the shadows of the trees gave way to the bright sunlight of a grassy meadow. Flowers dotted the tall grass, waving gently in the soft breeze.

Enchanted by the sight, Red Hawk moved silently across the meadow. He noticed that there was not a single trail in the grass. No sign of a crushed blade of grass or even one small feather met his gaze. It was as if no living creature had ever been there.

Then Red Hawk's sharp eyes settled upon an even more curious sight. In the middle of the meadow, a circular path was worn into the grass.

"Who has been here?" wondered the young man.

Red Hawk looked around closely, seeking the answer to his question. He saw no sign of footsteps leading to the circle, nor any leading away from it. For a hunter of Red Hawk's skill, the mystery was irresistible.

"I must find out who or what has made this strange ring," he said. Going back to the forest, Red Hawk hunted a bird for his supper. Then he disguised himself in the bird's feathers. Returning to the meadow, he hid in the tall grass and quietly waited.

Soon his patience was rewarded. Red Hawk heard faint music. The sweet strains came from above, and they sounded as if they were getting closer. He looked up but could see nothing except a small dark spot far up in the clouds. The tiny dot was floating down to earth. Closer and closer it came. At last, Red Hawk saw that the dot was an intricately woven basket. In it were beautiful maidens, each more lovely than the next.

The basket landed softly within the circular path. Out jumped the sky maidens. When the women began to dance on the path around the basket, moving in time to the high, sweet music, the basket rose above their heads and changed into a shining silver star. As the women danced around and around the circle, they drummed a rhythm upon the star with long willow branches.

As Red Hawk admired their pretty dance, his eyes settled upon the youngest girl. "Never have I seen such beauty and grace," he thought. Impulsively, Red Hawk ran from his hiding place, grasping the arm of the youngest maiden, whose name was Morning Star.

The frightened girl cried out. "Quickly, sisters, we must go!" shouted the oldest girl. Morning Star pulled herself free from Red Hawk's hold and she and all her sisters jumped into the basket. Like a bird taking flight, the basket rose quickly into the sky and disappeared from sight.

Cursing his clumsiness, Red Hawk looked at the worn path. "I have ruined everything," he moaned. "I will never see her again."

Red Hawk returned to his lodge that night. Sitting by the fire, he could think of nothing but Morning Star. He decided that he would go back to the circle the next day. That night a woodchuck came to Red Hawk in his dreams and offered to help him.

The following morning when Red Hawk awoke he used his dream to change himself into a woodchuck. He hurried to the circular path and hid near the edge of the forest.

Once again music filled the air. As before, the basket descended, carrying its lovely passengers.

Light as feathers, the women hopped upon the path and began their mysterious dance. Red Hawk crept closer and closer, dragging himself through the grass on his stomach as a woodchuck would do.

"Look at that strange animal," called Morning Star to the others.

"Perhaps he has something to show us," said the oldest sister.

But Morning Star sensed danger. "No!" she cried. "We must go!"

As quickly as they had hopped out of the basket, the women leaped back into it. Chanting together in high voices, the sisters held hands, and the basket rose into the sky.

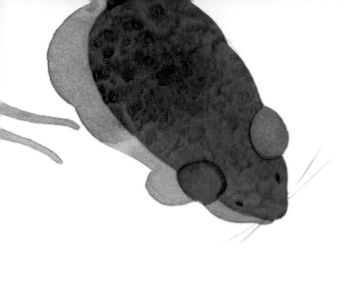
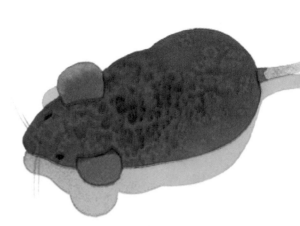

Although he was disappointed that his plan had failed, Red Hawk could not forget the beautiful face and graceful dancing of Morning Star. So he devised another plan.

"Surely she will not be afraid of a creature as small as a mouse," he said. The next day he searched the forest until he had found a den full of mice. Catching the mice, he put them in a hollow tree stump. Then he pulled the stump out of the ground and carried it to the meadow.

Placing the stump near the circular path, Red Hawk sang a mouse-changing song and turned himself into a mouse. He scurried into the tree stump and waited there for the basket to arrive.

As before, the basket appeared, and the sisters began their dance. But very soon, Morning Star cried out in alarm. "Where did that tree stump come from?" she called to the others. "We are in danger!"

The others laughed at her. "Why are you afraid of a tree stump?" asked one. All but Morning Star took their sticks and began

to poke and hit the stump as if it were a drum. The frightened mice ran out, and the sisters chased them playfully. Soon all but one mouse had found its way to a hiding place.

The remaining mouse raced from one sister to the next, until it found Morning Star. When she bent close to let it climb onto her hand, the mouse suddenly changed, and Red Hawk stood there, tenderly holding the maiden in his arms.

Seeing this, the others fled into the basket and escaped. The couple was left far below, alone in the meadow.

"Do not be afraid," said Red Hawk. With all the love in his heart, he told Morning Star the many stories and adventures of his life as a hunter. He spoke of the beauty and mystery of the forest. He sang songs to her and prepared the finest food for her to eat. As they made their way through the forest to his lodge, Red Hawk bent back the branches of the trees to clear her a path. He set stones over streams and moved fallen logs to ease her way.

Morning Star came to love Red Hawk, and he felt himself to be the luckiest and happiest man on earth. The two lived in joy together. In time, Morning Star gave birth to a healthy and beautiful baby boy.

17

The seasons passed. Despite her love for Red Hawk, the young wife missed her home in the sky. She was the daughter of Bright Star, and she longed to see her father and sisters again.

"I must return to the sky," she told her little son. "I will take you with me so that you may see what a wonderful place it is." The woman knew a song chant that would carry her home. But first she would need to make a basket to carry her and her son.

For many days she worked in secret, weaving a large basket. As gifts for her father and sisters, Red Hawk's wife prepared special foods from the meat her husband brought home each day. These she hid in the basket, along with pretty shells and stones from the earth.

When all was ready, Morning Star waited for Red Hawk to go hunting. Then she gathered her son in her arms and climbed into the basket. Morning Star began singing in a high, clear voice. In wonder, the little boy felt the basket rising. Looking over the edge, he saw his earthly home growing smaller and smaller, until it was only a tiny speck.

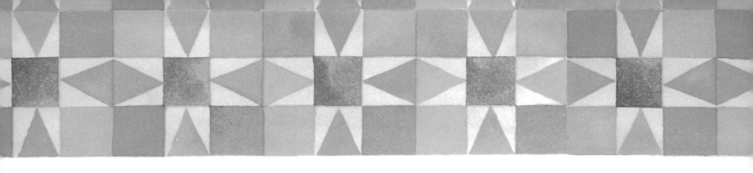

As the basket made its way upward, a mysterious song filled the air. It was the very same song Red Hawk had heard the first time he had ever seen his wife.

The music filled Red Hawk's ears as he came home from the day's hunt. His heart flooded with fear. "Is my wife gone?" he cried. Racing home, he found his lodge empty.

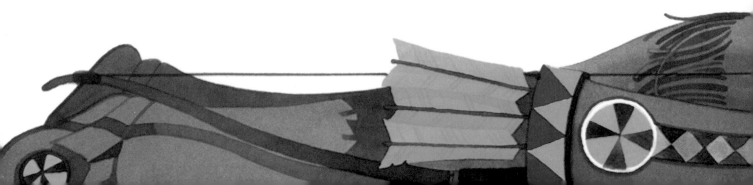

Fearing the worst, he called out for his son, but no one answered. Then, looking upward, he saw a tiny basket as it disappeared into the clouds. Heartbroken, Red Hawk fell upon the ground and wept.

Days turned to months, and months turned to years, but Red Hawk could not forget his loss.

Meanwhile, Red Hawk's wife was greeted by her father, Bright Star, and her sisters. Joyfully, they accepted the gifts she'd brought them from earth. They loved her little son very much and took good care of him.

But as the boy grew older, he often asked his mother and grandfather about the home he remembered. "Where is my father?" he asked sadly.

At last, Bright Star could no longer bear the boy's sadness. He called his youngest daughter to him. "Return to your husband on earth," he told her. "Take your son with you. You must tell your husband to come and live with us in our sky lodge. Before he does so, ask him to go hunting. He must kill one of each kind of bird and animal from the forest and bring them to me."

Red Hawk's wife did as her father told her. As she and her son descended to earth, they saw Red Hawk sitting in the meadow where he had first seen the mysterious circle. He often went there, his hawk eyes searching the skies, hoping for a glimpse of the basket that had carried his family away.

Red Hawk ran to them, eagerly reaching out to hug his family. Tears of joy flowed as they held each other once again. Morning Star explained what needed to be done. Red Hawk rejoiced at her words.

Eagerly, he set out for the hunt. Never had his senses served him so keenly, as he searched each part of the forest. With the patience and the skill of a hawk, he hunted each creature. From each one he kept a small part—a rabbit's tail, an owl's feather.

At last, all was ready. Red Hawk, his wife, and his son loaded their treasures into the basket and climbed in. One last time, Red Hawk heard the sweet music, as the basket ascended from the circle in the meadow to the star nation.

"Welcome," said Bright Star when the family reached the skies. He called all the star people together for a great celebration. After a fine feast, Bright Star laid out each of the gifts that Red Hawk had brought to him.

"Come," called Bright Star. "Each of you may take one of earth's treasures. Choose your favorite."

Everyone did so, eager to see what they might find. One chose a fox's tail and was instantly changed into a fox! Another chose a bear claw, and he became a bear! One by one, the guests chose a feather or a tail or a claw and then became that creature. Away they flew, scurried, or ran to the forests of earth.

As for Red Hawk and his wife and son, each chose a feather from a hawk. Immediately, they were transformed. Spreading their wide, strong wings, they flew down to the forest. And to this day, that is where you will find Red Hawk—reunited at last with his beloved wife and child.

The Shawnee

THE SHAWNEE

Shawnee Homeland

The Shawnee were nomads, which meant they were always on the move. Villages regularly broke into smaller bands to flee from attacking tribes such as the Iroquois, or to search for better farming or hunting land. Different bands have lived in fifteen states including Alabama, Georgia, and Pennsylvania. By the seventeenth century, many lived in the woodlands of the Ohio Valley along the Ohio and Scioto Rivers in Ohio and Kentucky.

Main villages were usually by fresh water and could have hundreds of "wegiwas." They were dome or square-shaped structures built with wooden pole frames and covered with bark or animal skins. Large villages also had a "msikamelwis," a large council house made of logs and used for ceremonies. The main village broke up in winter as groups of extended families moved around, hunting and trapping. Every spring, all the families gathered at the main village, where the women could tend to crops, usually just outside the village.

Above. A Shawnee wegiwas covered with mats made from reeds.

Shawnee People

Their name means "Southerners," in the Algonquian language, meaning that they were the southernmost group of the Algonquian speakers.

Men hunted, trapped, fished, traded, waged war, and built homes. Women raised crops and children, gathered food, took care of the homes, and preserved and prepared food. Children were welcomed and expected to help their elders. Daily cold-water baths were thought to strengthen babies.

Male chiefs ruled villages with a tribal council. Large villages would have many chiefs. The peace chief was the spiritual leader of the village—a position passed from father to son. War chiefs were great warriors. There were also female peace and war chiefs who were related to the male chiefs. All chiefs had equal voice in village business and worked together for the people.

One of the greatest war chiefs was Tecumseh. He lived during the late 1700s, when white settlers began moving into Shawnee homeland. Tecumseh worked hard to unite the many native tribes into a Native confederacy to fight encroaching white settlers. Together with his brother, Tenskwatawa, who was also called the Shawnee Prophet, Tecumseh lived along the Tippecanoe River in a camp called Prophet's Town. A gifted leader, warrior, and speaker, Tecumseh traveled far and wide urging other tribes to stop selling land and to unite into an alliance.

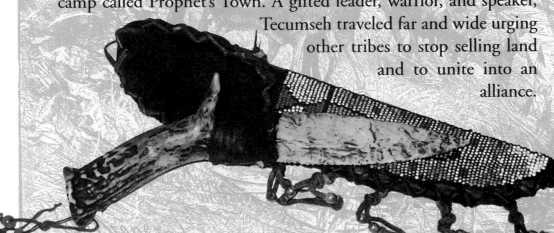

The powerful brothers soon had many followers. By 1811, warriors from many tribes lived in Prophet's Town. The governor of Indiana territory, William Henry Harrison, was quick to plan an attack. While Tecumseh was away, the Prophet fought a premature and losing battle against Harrison. Tecumseh returned to find Prophet's Town and his vision of a Native confederacy destroyed. He died in 1813 fighting for the British at the Battle of the Thames, hoping until the end that a British victory would mean peace for the Shawnee.

Bottom Left. Deer handle knives similar to this one were used by the Shawnee when hunting and fighting.

Right. Tecumseh was a great Indian warrior. His virtues -- honesty, helpfulness, dignity, and kindness -- were used as the basis for the Boy Scouts of America.

Bottom. Tecumseh's tomahawk pipe is beautifully decorated with silver.

Food and Clothing

Men hunted deer, buffalo, and turkey for meat. They also trapped smaller game such as raccoon, otter, and beaver both for food and for precious furs for trading. Men also fished, with spears or nets. Women gathered wild rice, berries, roots, herbs, and nuts. Women and children also planted and tended crops of corn, squash, beans, and pumpkins. Some groups made sugar from maple sap and had access to salt mines.

Clothing was usually made out of prepared animal skins, which were sometimes dyed or painted, and decorated with feathers or dyed porcupine quills. In summer, men wore a shirt and loincloth and women wore a long shirt. Leggings were added in winter for warmth. Both wore skin moccasins. Warriors usually wore a feather in their hair. Both sexes loved silver jewelry, like necklaces and bracelets, which they received in trade from Europeans.

Top. Ceramic pots, similar to this one from Kentucky, were made by the Shawnee up to the mid-1700s. Archeologists have found entire pots buried with their owners.

Right. Shawnee from left to right, Chief Kishkalwa, warrior Paytakootha, and Tecumseh's brother Prophet Tenskwatawa. Note the pierced ears and noses.

SCIOTO RIVER

Bank 60 ft high

Area 20 Acres

250 ft.

d

Dug holes

d

d

d

Area 18 Acres

d

Low Bottom Land.

Natural Bank 50 ft. high

a

b

Dug holes

d

d

Dug holes

Background. A map of earthen mounds that were built in Ross County, Ohio. These were possibly built by the ancestors of the Shawnee as temple sites.

d

d

B

300 Ft.

Shawnee Today

Today the Shawnee people are divided into three major groups: the Absentee Shawnee Tribe, the Eastern Shawnee Tribe, and the Loyal or Cherokee Shawnee Tribe. They live in cities and towns with non-natives, and on reservations in Oklahoma and Ohio. Many celebrate the old ways through dance and ceremonies while working in non-native professions such as law, education, and the arts.

Top. Shawnee Chief Alford and his family in Shawnee, Oklahoma, in the early 1900s.

Left. This stone hammer head is similar to those used by the Shawnee ancestors.

Top. This Indian dancer is similar to Shawnee dancers.

Right. The Shawnee used beautiful patterns similar to this as decorations to their clothing and blankets.

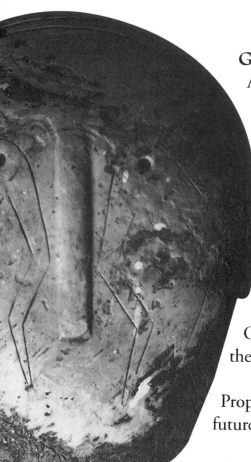

Glossary

Alliance: People or groups who join together for the same goal

Confederacy: A union of many groups that act as one group with a common goal

Msikamelwis: A large log structure for social ceremonies

Nomads: People who move from place to place

Our Grandmother: A female deity worshipped as the Creator by the Shawnee

Prophet: Someone who people believe can foresee future events

Roach: A headdress worn by men, usually made out of deer or porcupine hair and a few feathers

Wegiwas: Dome or square-shaped structures with wooden pole frames covered in bark or animal skins

Top. A crying eye design on a conch shell mask found in the 1930s at an archeological site near the Ohio River. This mask is similar to those used by the ancestors of the Shawnee.

Bottom. The home of the famous Shawnee artist Ernest Spybuck in 1928.

Above. A young Shawnee chief in Tulsa, Oklahoma, dressed for a special occasion.

Right. A two headed stone pipe similar to this was used by the ancestors of the Shawnee in Ohio.

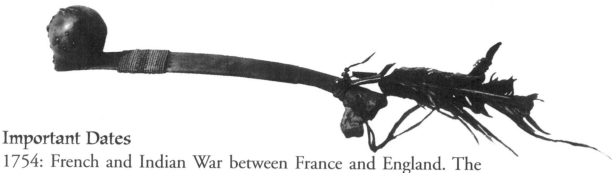

Important Dates

1754: French and Indian War between France and England. The Shawnee side with the French.

1768 (?): Tecumseh is born.

1776: American Revolution between England and the colonists. The Shawnee side with the British.

1795: Greenville Treaty is signed by the U.S. government and natives representing 12 tribes. The treaty opened the Shawnee homeland to white settlement. Tecumseh refused to attend the meeting.

1808: Prophet's Town is established along Tippecanoe River.

1811: Major General William Henry Harrison's troops destroy Prophet's Town at the Battle of Tippecanoe, effectively ending native resistance in the Ohio Valley.

Top. War club similar to those used by the Shawnee.

Right. Shawnee used arrowheads similar to these to hunt deer, porcupine, turkey, and other animals.

1812: War of 1812 between America and England. Tecumseh joins the British hoping a British victory will return the homeland to the Shawnee.

1813: Tecumseh is killed in the Battle of the Thames.

1840: William Henry Harrison is elected the 9th President of the United States. His campaign slogan "Tippecanoe and Tyler, Too" refers to the victory at Tippecanoe and John Tyler, his vice president.

1924: All Native Americans born in the U.S. are declared citizens.

1968: Indian Civil Rights Act gives Native Americans the right to govern themselves on their reservations.

Above. Shawnee kindergarten children dressed in their school clothes.

PHOTO CREDITS

We want to extend a special thank you to Chester R. Cowen, from the Archives & Manuscript Division of the Oklahoma Historical Society, for all of his help in acquiring images for this book.

Pages 32-33: Sky, Photo by Dave Albers
              A Bird Creek Shawnee, June 16, 1908, Cropped, Cherokee Strip Museum Collection,
              Courtesy of the Oklahoma Historical Society, #1001G
Pages 34-35: Map by Susan Albers; Wegiwas, Illustration by Dave Albers
Pages 36-37: Knife, Photo by Dave Albers; Deer and Tecumseh, Illustrations Courtesy of a Private Collection
              Tecumseh tomahawk, Courtesy of the Ohio Historical Society
Pages 38-39: Pot, Outlined, Courtesy of the William S. Webb Museum of Anthropology, University of Kentucky
              Three Shawnee, Outlined, McKenney-Hall 1837 lithos, Courtesy of the Oklahoma Historical Society,
              Left to Right the 1st two were painted by Charles Bird King, 3rd was painted by James Otto
              Lewis, #20516.1.3, #20516.1.18, #20699.821
              Background Map, Courtesy of a Private Collection
Pages 40-41: Family (Photo by Willis E. Brooks) and Dancer (Photographer's #2), Both Cropped and Dancer
              Tinted, Courtesy of the Oklahoma Historical Society, #637, #12817
              Stone Hammer, Photo by Dave Albers, Courtesy of a Private Collection
              Pattern, Dover Books
Pages 42-43: Mask, Outlined and tinted, Courtesy of the William S. Webb Museum of Anthropology,
              University of Kentucky
              House and Chief, Both Cropped and Chief Tinted, House from Anna W. Lewis Collection in
              Kickapoos and Chief from Photographer's #52, Courtesy of the Oklahoma Historical Society,
              #20744.1, #12816
              Stone pipe, Courtesy of a Private Collection
Pages 44-45: War Club and Arrowheads, Photos by Dave Albers. Arrowheads handcrafted by Eddie Albers,
              Courtesy of a Private Collection; Pattern, Dover Books
              Children, Cropped and Tinted, Gilstrap Collection, Courtesy of the Oklahoma Historical
              Society, #14540
Pages 47-48: Two Shawnee men, Courtesy of the Oklahoma Historical Society, #3440
              Earthen mound, Courtesy of a Private Collection

BIBLIOGRAPHY

Brandon, Alvin M. The American Heritage Book of Indians. New York: American Heritage Publishing Co., 1961.

Clark, Jerry E. The Shawnee. Lexington, KY: University Press of Kentucky, 1977.

Connell, Kate. These Lands Are Ours: Tecumseh's Fight for the Old Northwest. Austin, TX: Raintree Steck-Vaughn Publishers, 1993.

Hubbard-Brown, Janet. The Shawnee. New York: Chelsea House Publishers, 1995.

O'Neill, Laurie A. The Shawnees. Brookfield, CT: Millbrook Press, 1995.

Schraff, Anne. Tecumseh: The Story of an American Indian. Minneapolis, MN: Dillion Press, 1979.

Sturtevant, William C., General Editor. Handbook of North American Indians: California (Volume 8). Washington: Smithsonian Institution, 1978.

Waldman, Carl. Encyclopedia of North American Tribes. New York: Facts on File, 1988.

White, Jon Manchip. Everyday Life of the North American Indian. New York: Holmes & Meier, 1979.